I0755008

DEALING WITH...
DIFFICULT PEOPLE
AIMEE POPALIS
Mitchell Lane
PUBLISHERS

Parent and Caregiver Tips for Creating Nonfiction Readers

Timely topics in the *Dealing With...* series will interest intermediate and middle school readers and equip them with helpful strategies for coping with difficult situations. Your reader will be introduced to new concepts, facts, ideas, and vocabulary.

Tips for Reading Nonfiction

Talk about Nonfiction

Explain that nonfiction books provide facts about real-world topics. When readers read nonfiction, they gain a rich understanding of the world. They build background knowledge that provides a foundation for learning and academic success.

Look at the Parts

This book contains the following helpful features. Share the purpose of each feature with your reader.

Photos, Captions, and Graphic Aids
The photos, captions, charts, and other graphic aids in nonfiction texts contain a wealth of information. Help your reader identify different ways information can be displayed.

Sidebars
These extra tidbits of information help satisfy readers' curiosity and expand their knowledge.

Table of Contents
Located at the front of the book, this list shows the big ideas within the text and the page numbers where they can be found.

Extension Activities and Additional Resources
A "Your Turn" quiz and "Exploration and Discovery" activities invite readers to apply their new knowledge. Supporting resources are provided in a special "You Are Not Alone" section.

Glossary
Located at the back of the book, the glossary defines key words and phrases that are related to the topic. These words and phrases can be found in the text in **bold** type.

Index
Located at the back of the book, the index is an alphabetical list of topics and the page numbers where they can be found.

With a little help and guidance, your reader will be on their way to enjoying and learning from nonfiction books.

Mitchell Lane
PUBLISHERS

mitchelllanepub.com

2001 SW 31st Avenue
Hallandale, FL 33009

Copyright © 2026 by Mitchell Lane Publishers. All rights reserved. No part of this book may be reproduced without written permission from the publisher. Printed and bound in the United States of America.

First Edition, 2026.
Author: Aimee Popalis
Designer: Rhea Magaro
Editor: Kim Thompson

Series: Dealing With...
Title: Dealing with Difficult People / by Aimee Popalis

Hallandale, FL : Mitchell Lane Publishers, [2026]

Library bound ISBN: 979-8-89260-671-4
eBook ISBN: 979-8-89260-682-0

PHOTO CREDITS
Dreamstime: Gunold, 5, 41; Shutterstock: Prostock-studio cover, 1, 35; BearFotos, 7; M. Rohana, 8; Andrii Iemelianenko, 9; MiniStocker, 10; Ground Picture, 11; Ariya J, 13; Wirestock Creators, 14; Asier Romero, 15; Julia Zavalishina, 17; Veja, 19; sutadimages, 20; Dragana Gordic, 21; cheapbooks, 22; Vector Tradition, 23; CreativeAngela, 24; Ground Picture, 25; solar22, 26; catocala7, 30; Melnikov Dmitriy, 31; Lopolo, 32; Motortion Films, 34; ArtDarya, 35; Media_Photos, 36; digitalskillet, 37; Teechai, 38; iofoto, 42; SrideeStudio, 44; Anna Om, 47

Table of Contents

Chapter 1: Drama on and off the Stage

Sophia

Sophia dropped her backpack on the floor. She collapsed onto the sofa with a groan.

"Tough day?" her brother asked.

"I'm quitting the play," Sophia huffed.

"Why? You were so excited to get the part!"

"I was, but Tyler is ruining it. He only cares about his ideas. He talks over me, criticizes my performance, and orders everyone around. I leave rehearsals feeling like I can't do anything right."

"Is he like that with everyone?" Sophia's brother asked.

"Everyone!" Sophia insisted. "No one shares ideas because Tyler shoots them down. Nobody is having fun. I don't know what his problem is. I can't stand it anymore."

What Do You Think?

- How does Tyler's behavior affect Sophia's feelings about being in the play?
- How could Sophia deal with Tyler's behavior without quitting the play?
- Have you ever had to work with a difficult person? What did you do?

Chapter 2: What Is Difficult Behavior?

Sometimes, people act in ways that make it hard to get along. Even kind people can have moments when their behavior makes situations tricky. There are also people who just seem to be difficult most of the time.

Handling interactions with people like this can be tricky. It helps to learn why someone acts the way they do.

It's important to remember that someone who makes bad choices isn't necessarily a bad person. They may not even realize how their behavior affects others. Often, challenging behaviors happen because someone doesn't know how to express their feelings or ask for what they need. It's not because they want to upset others.

Did You Know?

One of the oldest records of a conflict was written in Egypt in 2500 BCE. It describes an argument between two neighbors over land boundaries.

Types of Difficult Behavior

There are many difficult behaviors. Most fall into four categories.

Aggressive Behavior

People who act with **aggression** always seem ready to fight. They often lash out at others. They may be:

- Physically Aggressive: They cause physical pain or threaten to cause pain. They may hit or throw things.
- Verbally Aggressive: They cause emotional pain. They may shout or say hurtful things.
- Passive-Aggressive: They say or do hurtful things but pretend they are not mad at all. They might make **sarcastic** or sneaky comments instead of speaking up directly.

Did You Know?

It is never okay to hurt or threaten others. You can deal with aggressive behavior by:

- Refusing to fight back.
- Encouraging the person to communicate calmly.
- Getting help from a trusted adult.

Did You Know?

You can deal with negative behavior by:

- Refusing to take the behavior personally.
- Not trying to cheer the person up.
- Asking to hear the person's positive ideas or solutions.
- Staying focused on what you can control.

Negative Behavior

People who act in negative ways fail to support others. They might make people feel bad about themselves. They may be:

- Complaining or **Pessimistic**: They focus on what's wrong instead of being positive.
- Critical or Judgmental: They point out others' mistakes or act like a know-it-all.
- Drama-Seeking or Gossiping: They enjoy stirring up problems or spreading rumors.

Did You Know?

You can deal with controlling behavior by:

- Refusing to let the person make all of the decisions.
- Trying to find a compromise.
- Being kind but firm about your **boundaries**.

Controlling Behavior

People who act in controlling ways pay more attention to what they want than to what others want. They try to control people and situations. They may be:

- Bossy or Stubborn: They refuse to **compromise** or listen to others.
- Manipulative: They use others to get what they want.
- Selfish: They think only of themselves and ignore others' needs or feelings.

Disengaged Behavior

People who act in disengaged ways seem like they don't care. They don't try to interact with others or make a difference. They may be:

- Unmotivated: They aren't interested in the group's goals or in helping others.
- Silent: They don't talk or share ideas, making teamwork difficult.

Did You Know?

You can deal with disengaged behavior by:

- Not trying to force the person to participate.
- Being patient and allowing the person to take part when they're ready.
- Suggesting simple activities and asking questions that require more than a *yes* or *no* answer.

Difficult People and Individual Differences

There are many reasons why people behave in difficult ways. Often, their actions are caused by a **trigger**, or something that upsets them. Everyone's triggers are different. A person's triggers are as personal as their favorite foods or music.

Understanding what's causing someone's difficult behavior can help you have **empathy** for them. It can help you see the situation from their **perspective**. Common triggers for difficult behaviors include:

- ☐ Having strong emotions
- ☐ Having low **self-esteem**
- ☐ Experiencing **stress**
- ☐ Going through changes with family or friends
- ☐ Being tired, hungry, or in pain
- ☐ Seeing that others don't care
- ☐ Having a brain that works differently than other people's

WARNING!
Triggers
Ahead

Studies Show That...

Bonobos, relatives of chimpanzees, solve conflicts with gentle touches, hugs, grooming each other, and sharing food.

Sometimes, someone else's difficult behavior triggers you. It's natural to feel upset when someone acts unkindly. But try to take a deep breath and think it through before you speak or act. Reacting without thinking can start a chain of negativity, just like knocking over a row of dominoes. Ask yourself these questions.

- What might be causing the person's behavior? Is something triggering them?
- How can I show empathy or improve the situation?
- Does understanding the person's feelings make it easier to handle their behavior?

Understanding triggers—your own and other people's—helps you respond with patience and kindness. It makes it easier to solve problems and build better relationships.

Recognizing Your Own Difficult Behavior

Difficult people often don't realize they are being difficult. That is true for other people. It is true for you too! Take time to think about your own behavior. Noticing how your feelings, words, and actions affect others is called **self-awareness**. When you practice seeing yourself clearly, you can make better choices and avoid behaving in difficult ways.

There Is Good News!

Have you been difficult? Use these steps to make a good apology.

1. Admit what you did wrong.
   I'm sorry I yelled.
2. Take responsibility.
   It wasn't okay to lose my temper.
3. Acknowledge the impact on others.
   I know that I hurt your feelings.
4. Explain how you will improve.
   Next time, I will take a deep breath and speak calmly.

Chapter 3: Signs of Difficult Behavior

A difficult person is someone whose behavior feels hurtful, unfair, or frustrating to you. That's true even if others feel differently about the person. Common difficult behaviors include:

- ☐ Interrupting or not listening
- ☐ Blaming others or making excuses
- ☐ Refusing to share or cooperate
- ☐ Acting bossy or overly controlling
- ☐ Being mean or rude
- ☐ Ignoring the feelings or needs of others
- ☐ Lying or breaking promises

Ways that these behaviors can make you feel include:

- ☐ Upset, angry, or frustrated
- ☐ Worried or nervous
- ☐ Uncomfortable or pressured
- ☐ Disrespected or misunderstood
- ☐ Embarrassed, guilty, or unsure of yourself
- ☐ Physically ill (stomachache or headache)

Did You Know?

Frequent difficult behaviors can mean that someone is struggling to manage their emotions or doesn't understand how their words and actions affect others. The person deserves empathy, even if their actions are hard to understand.

Difficult People and Your Brain

When you must deal with challenging behavior, a part of your brain called the **amygdala** senses trouble. It causes you to feel strong emotions like anger or fear. Your heart may pound, and you may feel nervous or jumpy.

Usually, your brain's prefrontal cortex helps you make good choices. It reminds you to take deep breaths, use kind words, and think before acting. But if you are really upset, the amygdala can override your prefrontal cortex. This makes it harder to think clearly.

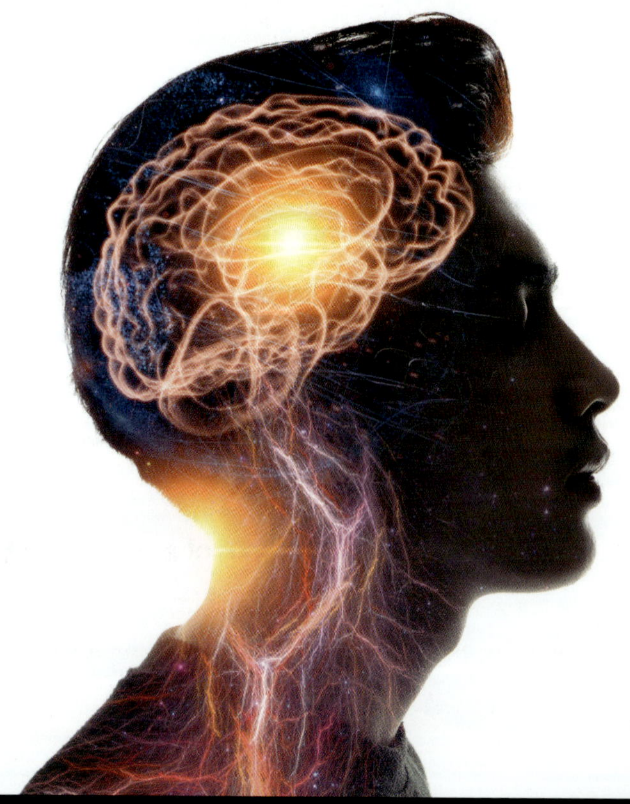

There IS Good News!

Mirror neurons are special nerves that help you understand how someone is feeling. They let you take one look at a person and know if they are happy or sad. If the person is angry or upset, your mirror neurons might cause you to feel that way too.

Dealing with difficult behavior causes stress. In response, your brain and body release the hormones **cortisol** and **adrenaline**. They prepare your body for action and put you in "fight-or-flight" mode. This can be helpful in an emergency. But if you're around difficult people too much, it can start to make you feel worn out.

Effects of Difficult Behavior

A person's difficult behavior can make you feel bad about yourself. It can lower your self-esteem. It may spoil activities you usually enjoy or make you want to avoid them altogether.

Difficult behavior doesn't just affect you. It also impacts how others in a group feel and act. It affects the group's dynamics, or the way people work together and get along. For example, if someone on a team is always negative or critical, it can lower **morale** and make others feel less excited to participate.

At first, the effects of difficult behavior might seem small and not that big of a deal. But, like a mosquito bite that won't stop itching, even tiny things can build up over time and become really uncomfortable.

Is This Normal?

With over eight billion people on Earth, it's normal to meet people that you find difficult. Even people you love, like friends or family members, sometimes act bossy, ignore your ideas, or say things that hurt your feelings.

Sometimes, people just don't get along. That's okay! You should always treat others with dignity and respect, even when they are difficult. But it is also important to have boundaries that protect your body and your emotions. Boundaries are rules or guidelines for how you expect to be treated by others. Boundaries help you decide what is okay and what's not. They make it easier to stand up for yourself.

Studies Show That...

Teams made up of people who have different perspectives often come up with better ideas and more creative solutions.

How can you tell if someone's difficult behavior is just a passing annoyance or a bigger problem? Pay attention to how often the behavior happens. Pay attention to how it makes you feel. Your observations will help you figure it out.

If someone's difficult behavior happens often and makes you feel scared, upset, or uncomfortable, it's a problem. For example, it's normal for a classmate to have strong opinions during a group project. But if the person refuses to listen to others, leaves you out, or says hurtful things, their behavior might be **toxic**.

Toxic behavior harms others by making them feel sad or afraid. Think of it like weather. A little wind is fine, but a tornado means that you need to take action to protect yourself. A trusted adult can help you decide what steps to take.

Chapter 4: Strategies for Taking Control

You can't control other people's behavior. But focusing on what you can control makes a big difference. Try these strategies for handling difficult people while reducing your stress, keeping your cool, and maintaining a positive outlook.

Strategy #1: Stand up for Yourself

Difficult people need to know how their behavior affects the people around them. Standing up for yourself in a calm, clear way puts them on alert. It helps everyone feel respected and understood. Try these techniques.

Studies Show That...

Standing up for yourself is good for your health! It reduces stress, lowers blood pressure, boosts your self-esteem, and helps you feel happier.

Use "I" Statements

Sometimes, people avoid standing up for themselves or setting boundaries because they fear it will start a conflict. Using "I" statements can help. It puts the focus on your feelings instead of on the other person's actions. Your words will sound more like sharing your perspective and less like picking a fight.

Instead of Saying...	Say...
You stole my turn!	I am frustrated that I missed my turn.
You hurt my feelings!	I feel sad when people talk to me like that.
You keep interrupting!	I don't like it when people talk over me.

Role-Play

It takes practice to feel confident and **assertive** while setting boundaries and standing up for yourself. Being assertive means communicating clearly and firmly without yelling or showing fear. Ask someone you trust to help you practice using "I" statements with a strong, steady voice and confident posture.

Strategy #2: Manage Your Emotions

Remember how conflict affects your brain? In stressful situations, your amygdala and prefrontal cortex battle for control. Staying calm allows your prefrontal cortex to win out. It helps you think critically and make good decisions. Try these techniques for staying calm and in control.

Butterfly Taps

This breathing exercise calms you down by involving both sides of your brain. Follow these steps.

1. Cross your arms over your chest with your hands on opposite shoulders.
2. Tap your shoulders in a slow rhythm, alternating left, right, left, right.
3. Match your breathing to the taps. Breathe in for four taps, then breathe out for four taps.
4. Keep the taps gentle and steady. Continue until you feel calm.

Traffic Light

1. Red: Stop and name your feeling.
   I'm feeling angry!
2. Yellow: Identify what caused the feeling.
   I'm angry that my partner wouldn't listen to my idea, because I was really excited about it.
3. Green: Decide how to respond.
   I need to talk to my partner and explain why this is important to me.

Strategy #3: Develop Empathy

Having empathy for someone means understanding their point of view. Active listening helps you develop empathy by really listening to someone and thinking about their perspective. Even if you don't agree with the person, active listening helps you understand them better and makes it easier to solve problems together. Follow these steps.

1. Look at the person. Show them you're paying attention.
2. Stay calm and quiet. Listen without interrupting.
3. Nod or say *okay*. Let them know you are hearing them.
4. Ask questions. If you don't understand, ask for more information.
5. Repeat back what they said. Say, "So you mean..." to make sure you got it.

Try to remember that people often act badly because they're having a tough time, not because of you. Acknowledge their feelings while making it clear how they should treat you. Say calmly, "I know you're upset, but that hurt my feelings. Let's talk more when you're feeling better." Caring about others doesn't mean accepting their unfair behavior.

Strategy #4: Break the Pattern

Sometimes, difficult behavior becomes a habit. Break the person's pattern by responding differently than you usually do. If you often argue, stay calm. If you usually ignore the person, point out how their actions make you feel. If you typically laugh it off, respond seriously. Changing your reaction can help the person see you, and their own behavior, differently.

It will also help you to learn from others. Find someone who stays confident, calm, and kind around difficult people. Pay attention to how they listen and set boundaries. Notice their tone of voice. Notice their posture and body language. Studying their approach can help you find what works best for you.

Strategy #5: Get Support

Sometimes, you need help dealing with difficult people. Turn to people you trust and admire. They've learned from their successes and mistakes and can share ideas to help you. They can also remind you that difficult people are a normal part of life, and that you're not alone in dealing with them.

If someone in a group is causing problems, talk privately with your teacher or coach. They understand how to handle different personalities. They might offer new solutions or plan ways to help the group work through challenges together.

There IS Good News!

Conflict can be exhausting. It can leave you wondering if you are the problem. Spending time with positive people boosts your confidence and your mood. It reminds you that you are awesome just as you are!

Strategy #6: Take Care of Yourself

Dealing with difficult people makes you tense. Being filled with stress-related hormones makes you feel restless. Moving your body can help! Try running, dancing, or walking your dog to release extra energy.

You can also try calming activities like deep breathing, drawing, or writing. These help you express your emotions and process your feelings. Take time to listen to music or read for pleasure. It will give your brain a break and make you feel ready to handle tough situations.

Studies Show That...

Getting outside reduces stress and improves your mood. Research shows that fresh air, sunlight, and being surrounded by nature helps you feel calmer and happier.

Chapter 5: Dealing with Difficult People

Remember Sophia? She was still upset about Tyler when her brother gave her some advice. "I felt the same way about a kid on my soccer team," he said. "But I found out he was dealing with tough times at home. Once I understood, I felt more patient. I knew the way he was acting wasn't about me or the team."

"Hmm. You think there's something behind Tyler's behavior?" Sophia asked.

"Maybe," her brother said. "His older sister was really good at theater. Tyler might feel pressure to be just as good."

At the next rehearsal, Tyler criticized Sophia's idea. She took a deep breath and said calmly, "Why do you think your idea will work better?" She listened closely to Tyler's response. She said, "Okay, let's try your way first, then mine."

To Sophia's surprise, Tyler agreed. Afterward, Sophia thought he seemed a little easier to get along with. Sophia was proud of herself for handling things in a new way. She knew that her teamwork with Tyler—and the play—would be stronger for it.

Remember: Difficult behavior is...difficult! Try to find a balance between your own boundaries and the needs of the other person. It will help you work together and find a peaceful solution.

YOUR TURN: HOW DO YOU DEAL WITH DIFFICULT PEOPLE?

For each situation, select the answer most likely to produce the best outcome. Make a note of your answers on a separate sheet of paper.

1. Layla's teammate blames her for losing the game. How should Layla respond?
   - **A.** Argue back. Her teammate's performance wasn't perfect either.
   - **B.** Take a deep breath and calmly say, "I understand you are upset about losing. Blaming me isn't helpful. We all tried our best."
   - **C.** Ignore her teammate. She's not worth the time.

2. Chris and his brother usually argue about whose turn it is to play a video game. How can Chris make it easier to share fairly?
   - **A.** Say, "I know it is important to both of us to have a turn. Let's agree to use a timer to make sure we both get fair turns every time."
   - **B.** Say, "I feel angry when I don't get a turn. Please share."
   - **C.** Let his brother have extra turns but feel frustrated and angry every time.

3. Aria's mom gets frustrated when helping Aria with her homework. How can Aria respectfully handle the situation?
   - **A.** Say, "I am trying. It is harder for me when you yell. Let's take a break and come back to it more calmly."
   - **B.** Shut down and stop trying.
   - **C.** Yell back and storm off.

4. Derrin insists on copying his friend Trey's homework, making Trey feel uncomfortable and a little upset. How can Trey handle Derrin's demand?
   - **A.** Let him copy anyway. He knows this subject is challenging for Derrin.
   - **B.** Agree to let Derrin copy, but then change all of his answers so Derrin gets them wrong. He won't want to copy again.
   - **C.** Tell Derrin he's not okay with people copying his work. Offer to meet up after school to help Derrin study and finish his homework.

Think about your answers.

1. The best answer is B. Taking a deep breath helps Layla be able to calmly show empathy and create a boundary with her teammate. She acknowledges that her teammate is upset, but she doesn't allow her to lay the blame on others.
2. The best answer is A. Creating an agreement to use a timer is a fair strategy that breaks the pattern of arguing and allows both brothers to have equal turns.
3. The best answer is A. Aria's calm and clear communication helps Aria's mom see that her behavior is becoming a problem. Suggesting a break gives both of them time to de-stress and come back to the assignment with more patience.
4. The best answer is C. Setting a boundary helps Trey stand up for what he knows is right. Offering to help Derrin study gives his friend the assistance he actually needs and may help them both avoid this situation in the future.

EXPLORATION AND DISCOVERY: ACTIVITIES TO TRY

1. Practice strengthening your voice. Stand in front of a mirror. Practice speaking clearly and firmly while saying phrases such as *I don't like that* or *Why do you say that?* Use confident posture, keep a neutral facial expression, and make eye contact.
2. Research someone who had to work with difficult people to get what they wanted. Find current or historical figures like Susan B. Anthony, Thor Heyerdahl, Serena Williams, or LeBron James. What strategies did they use to deal with difficult people? What lessons did they learn?
3. Play the compliment game. With a friend or family member, take turns giving each other sincere compliments. See how many good and kind things you can notice about them. Level up by playing with a person you are challenged to get along with. Find one thing about them you can truthfully appreciate.
4. Practice empathy. Think of a villain from a movie or book. What might be motivating their behavior? What do they want? What do they want to avoid? What would be a better way to get what they want? What might you say to them to acknowledge their feelings but draw a boundary for their behavior?

YOU ARE NOT ALONE

Dealing with difficult people can make you feel hopeless and alone. But you are NOT alone. There are good people who care about you and want to help. There are also many resources you can use to learn more and help yourself.

Explore some of these ways to find the kindness and support you deserve.

People to Ask for Help

☑ guidance counselor
☑ teacher
☑ principal
☑ assistant principal
☑ parent
☑ older sibling
☑ grandparent
☑ aunt or uncle
☑ coach
☑ school secretary
☑ bus driver
☑ religious youth group leader
☑ any friend that you trust
☑ any adult that you trust

Websites

Kids Help Phone: Arguing with a friend? Here's how to fight fair.
kidshelpphone.ca/get-info/arguing-friend-heres-how-fight-fair
Discover how to resolve a disagreement with a friend and move forward.

KidsScape: How can I be assertive and stand up for myself?
kidscape.org.uk/advice/advice-for-young-people/how-can-i-be-assertive-and-stand-up-for-myself
Learn how to be assertive and stand up for yourself with confidence.

Nemours TeensHealth: Assertiveness
kidshealth.org/en/teens/assertive.html
Find out how to communicate assertively and set healthy boundaries.

Books

Daniels, Natasha. *Social Skills Activities for Kids: 50 Fun Exercises for Making Friends, Talking and Listening, and Understanding Social Rules*. Callisto Kids, 2019.

Gladdin, Kate. *The Teen's Guide to Social Skills: Practical Advice for Building Empathy, Self-Esteem, and Confidence*. Callisto Teens, 2021.

Stephenson, Catherine. *Emotional Intelligence for Kids Workbook: Understanding Feelings, Self-Regulation and Mindfulness*. Wooden House Books, 2023.

Phone Helplines

Crisis Text Line
Text HOME to 741741 or message on WhatsApp. Young people of color can text STEVE to 741741 to reach culturally trained counselors.

LGBT National Youth Talkline
1-800-246-7743

National Suicide Prevention Lifeline
1-800-273-8255

Suicide and Crisis Lifeline
Call or text 988.

GLOSSARY

adrenaline (uh-DREN-uh-lin)

A chemical released in your body when you need more energy or when you sense danger

aggression (uh-GRESH-un)

Fierce, violent, or threatening behavior

amygdala (uh-MIG-duh-luh)

A small, almond-shaped part of your brain that plays a role in processing emotions, especially fear and anger

assertive (uh-SER-tiv)

A way of speaking or acting with confidence and purpose

boundaries (BOUN-dur-eez)

Rules you set for yourself to help you feel safe and respected

compromise (KAHM-pruh-mize)

To agree to accept something that is not entirely what you wanted in order to satisfy some of the requests of other people

cortisol (KOR-tuh-suhl)

A chemical produced by the adrenal glands when the body is under stress

empathy (EM-puh-thee)

Understanding and being sensitive to the feelings, thoughts, and emotions of others

morale (muh-RAL)

The confidence, enthusiasm, and teamwork of a group

perspective (pur-SPEK-tiv)

The way you see, experience, or understand something

pessimistic (PES-uh-mis-tik)

Always seeing the worst side of a situation or believing that the worst will happen

sarcastic (sahr-KAS-tik)

Using bitter or mocking words that are meant to hurt and make fun of someone or something

self-awareness (self-uh-WAIR-nis)

Knowing how you feel, what you think, and how your actions affect others

self-esteem (self-i-STEEM)

How you feel about yourself and how much you believe you're important and capable

stress (stress)

Worry, strain, or pressure

toxic (TAHK-sik)

Hurtful or damaging; poisonous

trigger (TRIG-ur)

Something that makes you feel strong emotions like anger, fear, or sadness

INDEX

ABOUT THE AUTHOR

Aimee Popalis didn't always know how to handle difficult people—in fact, as a kid, she had a hard time finding her assertive voice. (She mostly hoped the problem would go away.) Over time, she learned how to set boundaries and stand up for herself, though she admits she's still practicing! Now a teacher, Aimee loves helping kids tackle tough situations with humor and kindness. When she's not writing or teaching, you might find her paddling, crocheting, gardening, or making messes in her school's science lab. Aimee believes that with practice and courage, everyone can handle conflict with confidence and creativity!